200
Q&As
About
ANIMALS

Text by Cristina Banfi
Illustrations by Lorenzo Sabbatini

whitestar˙kids

CONTENTS

Our planet is inhabited by wonderful creatures, and it's easy to be enchanted by the extraordinarily rich, varied, and fascinating animal kingdom.

When observing wildlife, you have surely asked yourself several times: Why are those animals made that way? Why do some appear to possess **"superpowers"**? Why do others have such funny or unusual characteristics? And again, why does the behavior of some of them seem so extravagant, funny, and sometimes even crazy to us?

Are you curious about **nature**?

This fun book will help you find the answers to many *why* questions, and you will learn a lot of things about animals from all over the world.

You will discover that, very often, the appearance and the actions of an animal closely depend on the place where the animal lives—be it a forest, a desert, or an immense ocean—and those actions and appearances can be ingenious methods to escape predators, find food more easily, protect the young, and guarantee the survival of the species.

Would you like a tip?
Read carefully, because knowing what surrounds us is the first step in learning to respect, protect, and cherish our beloved Earth.

Forests and Jungles

Forests are not only the kingdom of plants. Many animals have established their homes in forests and are able to find everything they need there.

From the hot jungle to the cold snow forest, all animals that spend their lives in the trees or under their shade know how to survive.

They move, take care of their young, collect and store food, hide, and always find a safe shelter in the intricate maze of trunks, branches, and leaves.

Why do squirrels have a bushy tail?

The tail performs three main functions: it keeps the squirrel warm like a blanket, it is a means of communication with others, and it helps the squirrel to maintain its balance when it jumps from one branch to another.

Why do wolves howl?

They howl to communicate their position to the other members of their pack during a hunt.

Why do wolves howl at night?

Wolves rest during the day and go hunting in packs at night. Howling is more frequent and useful when they hunt.

Why can bats fly in the dark?

In total darkness, most bats use an exceptional way to orient themselves: they send ultrasounds that come back in the form of echoes when they hit an obstacle. By listening to them, the bat manages to avoid dangers!

Why is the vampire bat so called?

Like Count Dracula, this little bat feeds on blood; cows, pigs, and horses are its victims. Using its incisor teeth, the bat makes a small cut in the skin of the animal, which survives without being hurt.

Why do raccoons wash their food before eating it?

Actually, the raccoon does not clean its food but rather wets it to better understand what it is about to eat.

Why does the male peacock spread its feathers?

It's his way of getting a female's attention. During courtship, the male peacock arranges its gigantic tail feathers into a fan shape that vibrates, making the brightly colored patterns move: a real show-off!

Why does the female peacock have no colorful feathers?

The females are entrusted with the task of hatching the eggs and looking after the chicks. The brown color of their feathers helps to camouflage them, making them less visible to predators.

Why doesn't the cuckoo make a nest?

The cuckoo does not need to make a nest because it does not raise its young. The female secretly lays her eggs in other birds' nests, so that they unknowingly raise the little cuckoos for her.

Why are they called leafcutter ants?

These ants have particularly sharp jaws, which they use to cut small pieces of leaf. Then, they form a very long line and transport the pieces without stopping, from the top of the tree to their underground nest.

Why do leafcutter ants collect leaves?

The leaves decompose and are used to grow the mushrooms that ants are fond of.

Why does the anteater have no teeth?

Given what it eats, the anteater doesn't really need to chew its food, which is why its snout is long and narrow and its jaws are thin and toothless. The tongue, long and sticky, takes care of capturing its small prey.

Why does a deer shed its antlers?

A deer's antlers fall out every year as soon as the mating season ends.

Why doesn't a deer mind losing its antlers?

Losing antlers is fortunate for these animals as they will be able to grow even larger ones the following year.

Why do beavers make dams?

By wedging tree branches, beavers erect dams to block the flow of small rivers, thereby creating a lake. At the center of the lake, they build their lair, inside which they can live more peacefully, protected from wolves, coyotes, and pumas, who cannot reach them there.

Why does the crossbill have a crooked beak?

The beak of this bird looks malformed because the tips are crossed. It is the ideal tool to collect the pine nuts that the crossbill feeds on, as the beak is able to crack the pinecones open without much effort.

Why are baby deer born with spots on their backs?

At birth, a fawn has some light spots scattered on its back, which disappear with age. This coloring, imitating the combination of light and shadow of the undergrowth, makes the fawn invisible to predators, while it waits for its mother, hidden under a bush.

Why do wood frogs stop their hearts?

To survive the long, freezing winter, the frog hibernates. Thanks to an antifreeze substance in its blood, the frog can stop its heart and its breathing, while ice crystals form inside its body. In spring, it thaws and returns to activity.

Why does the dormouse have very large eyes?

When moving during the night, it is necessary to be able to see even in very low light. Its large eyes facilitate night vision and considerable help is also given by its mustache, which is very long: sensitive to the touch, it guides the way through the tree branches.

Why does the owl have a very quiet flight?

Active at night, the owl must hunt in absolute silence if it wants to be successful. For this reason, its wings have primary feathers with a "comb" edge that muffles the sound of the air as it flows over the surface of the wings.

Why does the jay hide seeds in the ground?

It is an ingenious way to store supplies in a safe place, hiding them from other animals' sight. The seeds are then recovered in the following days, but not all are found. That is why, thanks to the work of the jay, seeds are dispersed, which facilitates the birth of new plants.

Why does the owl have ears?

What you see popping up on the owl's head are not actually ears, but tufts of feathers that are not used for hearing. They help the owl to blend in with the branches and communicate with other owls. The "real" ears are two holes on the sides of the head hidden by feathers.

Why does the dormouse hibernate?

The low temperatures and the difficulty in finding food in winter do not allow this small mammal to survive. For this reason, when the first cold weather arrives, dormice roll up into a ball inside a nest made of grass and leaves, and enter a state of inactivity, becoming cold to the touch.

Why are orangutans so called?

The name means "man of the forest" in the local language of Borneo. According to legend, the orangutan was a human who climbed trees to avoid working.

Why do chameleons change their skin color?

They change color either to communicate their mood (if angry, for example, they become darker) or to control their body temperature. If it is hot, the color of their body lightens to reflect the heat of the sun.

Why do tigers have striped fur?

To hide in the jungle: the sun's rays filtering through the leaves creates strips of shadow similar to those of the tiger's coat.

Why do pythons yawn?

Not because they are tired: they are probably stretching their jaws, preparing to swallow prey, which can be as large as the width of their body.

Why does a python swallow prey whole, even very large prey?

Snakes are known to swallow their prey whole, even if large, by widening their mouth to twice the width of their head. The secret of how they do this lies in their jaws: they are loosely attached to the skull and positioned one on top of the other, joined only by an elastic ligament.

Why do anacondas live in water?

Due to their huge size, it is much easier for anacondas to swim in the water than to crawl slowly on land!

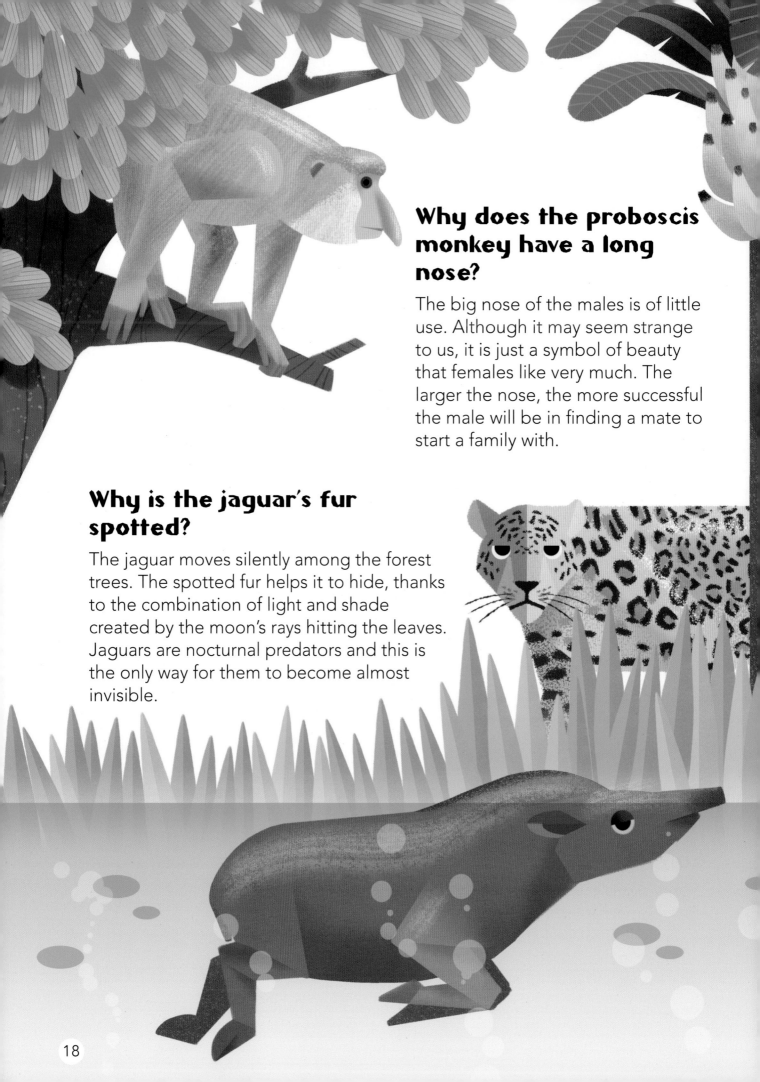

Why does the proboscis monkey have a long nose?

The big nose of the males is of little use. Although it may seem strange to us, it is just a symbol of beauty that females like very much. The larger the nose, the more successful the male will be in finding a mate to start a family with.

Why is the jaguar's fur spotted?

The jaguar moves silently among the forest trees. The spotted fur helps it to hide, thanks to the combination of light and shade created by the moon's rays hitting the leaves. Jaguars are nocturnal predators and this is the only way for them to become almost invisible.

Why do gibbons have long arms?

Swinging from tree to tree is a very useful adaptation skill for an animal living in a forest. This way of moving is typical of some primates with arms long enough to grab two distant branches, or to easily reach fruit to eat.

Why does the toucan have a large beak?

With such a large beak, toucans can easily pick even the largest fruit, which they catch and swallow after throwing it into the air. The beak also helps to control body temperature, because it dissipates the heat on hot days.

Why does the tapir have a trunk?

A long, flexible nose is very useful for collecting the plant shoots that the tapir eats. With it, the tapir can also sniff the ground to discover the odorous traces left by predators or other tapirs. If necessary, the trunk can become a snorkel for breathing underwater.

Why do sloths have long claws?

The sloth is a quiet animal that spends all day firmly clinging to a branch. The claws of all four limbs are very long and curved down toward the wrist, forming hooks, which allow the sloth to hang belly up without much effort.

Why do baby hoatzins have claws on their wings?

The young are born in a nest built in a tree. If there is a threat from a predator, the only way to escape is to drop into the water below. Once the danger has passed, the chicks return to the nest, climbing up the trunk, thanks to the small claws on their wings.

Why is the basilisk called the "Jesus Christ lizard"?

If it is looking for prey, or if it is disturbed and frightened, the basilisk straightens up on its hind legs and begins to run on the water, quickly moving to the opposite shore. It can travel up to 65 feet (20 m) before sinking.

Why is it called a howler monkey?

This monkey is one of the loudest animals in the world. Its howl can be heard from three miles away (5 km), and is as loud as the sound of a plane taking off.

Why does the howler monkey... howl?

It uses its powerful voice to mark its territory.

Why do parrots have two claws pointing forward and two pointing back?

This particular position of the claws is typical of birds climbing tree trunks, which all parrots can do very well! Using their scale-covered claws, they are also able to grasp and manipulate objects with skill.

Why do koalas eat only eucalyptus leaves?

Koalas only eat the leaves of eucalyptus trees, which are actually very low in protein and also toxic to many animal species. Being able to digest eucalyptus leaves is an advantage for koalas because they have a food source that is not in demand from other animals.

Why does the kiwi have short wings?

The kiwi has tiny wings, just 1.5 inches (3 cm) long, and is therefore unable to fly. It walks in the forest at night, looking for food and leaving its excrement around to mark its territory, which only its babies and its partner are allowed to enter.

Why does the cobra have a hood?

The unmistakable hood that all cobras possess appears when the snake spreads the skin on its neck. Cobras do this when they are disturbed or feel unsafe—the hood makes the head appear much larger than it really is, scaring enemies away.

Why does the lynx have long and sturdy hind legs?

The body of the lynx may appear a bit asymmetrical: the front legs are shorter and almost disproportionate compared to the hind legs, which are much longer and stronger. This characteristic is typical of animals that are good at jumping, which the lynx does to pounce on its prey.

Why does the panda live in the bamboo forest?

Pandas don't just eat bamboo leaves, although 99% of their meal is made of them. In bamboo forests, this plant is an abundant food for the panda; moreover, bamboo leaves are snubbed by most herbivorous animals.

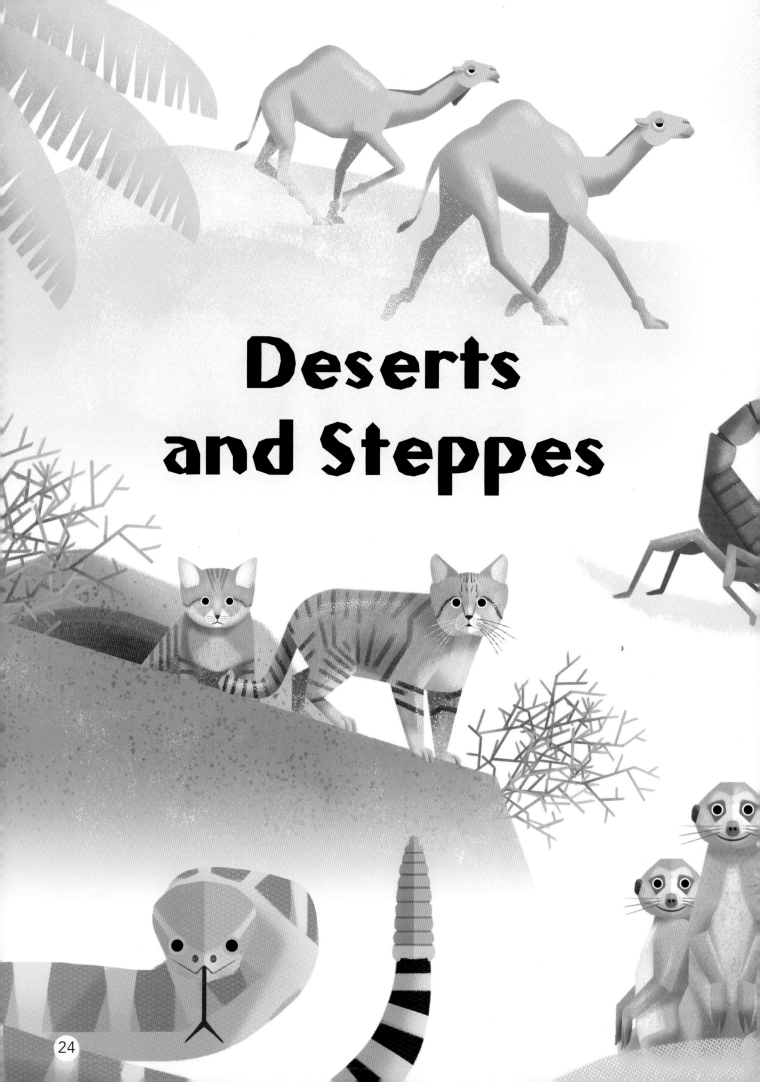

Deserts and Steppes

Living in a desert is not easy at all.
Since the heat is suffocating during
the day, it is more prudent to go
around at night to find food, when
the air becomes a little cooler.

The biggest problem, however, is the
scarcity of water, so the animals must
store it for as long as possible, avoiding
sweating and even never peeing.

In deserts, food is not abundant either.
There is no place here for fussy eaters.
Animals eat whatever they find, and
some even store fat in their body for
times of famine.

Why does the camel have humps?

Fat is stored in the camel's humps, which is used as a supply of energy, thereby allowing the camel to survive without food for several days.

Why do rattlesnakes have a rattle?

The rattle is on the tip of the tail and is made up of many rings of dry skin. As it is moved, the rings bang against each other, producing the characteristic sound. The rattlesnake uses the rattle to be recognized as a poisonous animal and, therefore, to be left in peace.

Why does the dromedary, despite being heavy, not sink into the sand?

The dromedary can walk and run in the desert, without sinking, thanks to its very wide hoofs, which rest on the ground, distributing the animal's weight evenly on the sand.

Why does the dromedary have long lashes?

The look of the dromedary is very sweet, especially because of the long lashes that embellish its large eyes. In actual fact, they prevent sand grains from entering the eyes during violent sandstorms.

Why is the wheel spider so called?

The wheel spider has invented an amazing way to escape predators as fast as possible: it catapults itself onto the sand and rolls away quickly, spinning on itself many times.

Why is the uromastyx also called the spiny-tailed lizard?

The name comes from its tail: large, short, and covered with big, pointed scales. The uromastyx uses it to protect itself and to block the entrance to its lair, which is dug into the ground.

Why does the Sahara sand viper move by sidewinding?

Crawling on the hot sand of the desert is not easy. For this reason, the Sahara sand viper makes sure that at any moment, only two points of its body touch the ground. The result is an oblique "wave" movement.

Why does the kangaroo rat have very long hind legs?

As you can imagine, the kangaroo rat does not walk, it jumps! It has huge hind legs, which allow it to make incredible 8-foot (2.5 m) leaps, which is the length of a motorcycle!

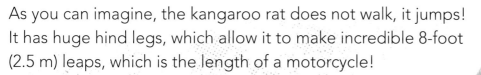

Why does the desert horned viper have two horns above the eyes?

The two small horns protruding from its head protect its eyes as the viper crawls around its world of sand.

Why can a shock be dangerous for the desert tortoise?

When it finds some water, this tortoise stores it up... in its bladder. However, if it gets frightened, it can involuntarily release the precious liquid and wet itself.

Why does the sand cat bark?

The sand cat is a solitary animal that seeks company only during the mating season. To find a mate, the male produces a sound that resembles a dog's barking.

Why does the saiga antelope have such a big nose?

This steppe antelope uses its large nose to filter the air and warm it, but its nose also functions as a megaphone, so its cry can be heard from far away.

Why does the pin-tailed sandgrouse collect drops of water among its chest feathers?

Its chest feathers are able to absorb small amounts of water. The males use them as a sponge to transport the precious liquid to their nests, where the young and their partner await them. This is the only way for them to quench their thirst.

Why does the oryx have a white back and black legs?

On hot days, the white coat of this large antelope is useful for reflecting sunlight. On the contrary, the dark color of its legs helps to absorb the faint heat of the morning, when it can get cold even in the desert.

Why does the addax antelope never drink?

It may seem strange to you, but the addax antelope does not really need to look for water sources because it does not need to drink. In fact, it is able to absorb all the humidity from the plants it feeds on and then uses it sparingly.

Why can geckos walk on vertical walls?

As skilled climbers, geckos walk effortlessly on walls and ceilings. The secret is in the adhesive pads they have on their fingertips. A light pressure keeps the gecko firmly attached to the wall while climbing.

Why do scorpions sting?

The scorpion has a stinger on the tip of its tail and can inject venom with it. It uses the stinger to hunt or as a defense when it feels threatened.

Why is the skink called a "sand fish" even though it is a lizard?

Its legs function like fins, and as it moves, it pushes the sand back with them, looking like it is swimming!

Why is the thorny devil lizard covered with thorns?

The thorns that cover the body of this lizard, in addition to protecting it and helping it hide, allow the few drops of humidity that land there in the morning to flow toward the mouth so that the lizard can drink.

Why does the fennec fox have big ears?

Big ears are certainly useful for hearing even the slightest sounds of a prey moving in the sand. However, the big size also helps to disperse the animal's body heat.

Why do kangaroos often lick their front legs on hot days?

Kangaroos cannot sweat and so they use a particular way to lower their body temperature: they lick their chest and the inside of their front legs, soaking their fur. As the saliva evaporates, the blood circulating underneath cools quickly.

Why do kangaroos have a pouch?

The pouch is a fold of skin that only females possess. It is used to protect and breastfeed joeys, which are very small at birth (just a few inches) and will remain inside the pouch until they reach 10 months.

Why do meerkats have dark spots around their eyes?

They appear to be wearing a mask but they are not robbers: the dark spots protect their sight by reducing the glare of the sun.

Why does the black vulture pee on its own legs?

On hot summer days, black vultures sometimes pee on their legs. They are not distracted; they are smart. When the water contained in their urine evaporates, it has a cooling effect.

Why does the cassowary have a casque on its head?

This strange casque could be of use to amplify the volume of the cassowary's sound, and also to protect the head when the animal runs in the thick of the forest.

Savannas
and Grasslands

Savannas and grasslands, where grass grows abundantly, are ideal places for antelopes, zebras, and many other herbivores, who gather here to form large herds.

And with so many herbivores come numerous carnivores. Some chase their prey, others take them by surprise, waiting to ambush.

Some animals dig underground burrows to protect themselves from predators or from the heat, and there are many who take advantage of the darkness of the night to hunt or to escape an attack.

Why does the oxpecker live on the body of large herbivores?

Oxpeckers perch on the backs of buffaloes, zebras, rhinos, and other large herbivores of the savanna to remove ticks, flies, and parasites from their skin. In addition to providing this cleaning service, oxpeckers warn their mammal "friends" of the arrival of predators.

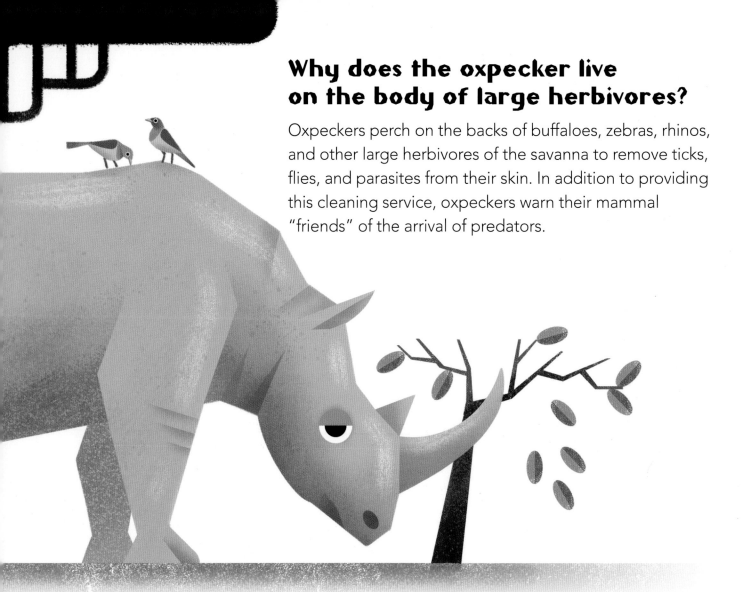

Why does the rhino have a horn on its nose?

The rhino horn is a dangerous weapon, as the animal constantly rubs it against rough surfaces, making it pointed and sharp. The rhino uses it for defense and also to dig into the soil in search of roots and to dig into the bed of dry rivers to find water.

Why do zebras have black-and-white striped bodies?

The stripes help the zebras repel parasitic insects, such as gadflies: it seems that the stripes disturb their landing maneuvers.

Why does the elephant have big ears?

Big ears are used by elephants to cool off: thanks to the numerous blood vessels, the blood cools them down, therefore lowering the temperature of the whole body.

Why do elephants have tusks?

Tusks are teeth that continue to grow throughout life. The elephant uses them for many things, such as digging holes, removing the bark from trees, and if necessary, even fighting. It even leans on its trunk when tired.

Why do giraffes have dark tongues?

Giraffes have purplish blue, almost black, tongues. Such a dark color is useful to protect the tongue from the sun's rays and prevents it from getting burned.

Why do giraffes have long necks?

The neck is certainly the most noticeable feature of the giraffe. Thanks to it, the giraffe manages to collect leaves from the highest branches, which other herbivores cannot reach. Males use their necks to fight each other, hitting their rival's belly with it.

Why do crocodiles cry after eating?

When crocodiles spend a lot of time out of the water, their eyes dry out and only by releasing tears can they become wet again. Of course, the crying is not due to remorse for the killed prey!

Why does the male lion have a mane?

Male lions proudly wear their mane to show how healthy and strong they are. The thicker and darker the mane, the more attractive it is to females, who will be able to choose the best father for their offspring.

Why does the lion have a very rough tongue?

Lions have a rough tongue, like sandpaper. It is covered with tiny backward-facing spines, very useful for scraping away the flesh of prey from its bones. Never let a lion lick your hand because it would leave you skinless in no time!

Why do lions roar?

Male lions use their powerful roar to scare off intruders, warning them that they are invading their territory, but also to warn the members of the herd of potential danger.

Why does the leopard carry its prey up a tree?

The leopard carries much heavier prey than its own weight into trees, dragging it up several feet above the ground. It's a clever, albeit tiring, way to protect a meal that it'll consume, undisturbed, for several days.

Why can't the cheetah slip?

The cheetah is the only feline that cannot retract its claws. Its claws therefore always remain completely exposed. This feature ensures that the paws stick to the ground and prevents the paws from sliding when it reaches high speeds.

Why does the mole not have good eyesight?

The life of a mole takes place mainly underground, in total darkness, digging tunnels to catch food that it detects by smell. In its world, having good eyesight isn't necessary at all.

Why do gazelles live in large groups?

Gazelles, impalas, and many other herbivores live in herds of up to 700 individuals. By grazing, drinking, and sleeping all together, they have a better chance that one of them will notice the presence of a predator and give a signal to the rest of the group to flee.

Why does the pronghorn have a very large heart and large lungs?

The pronghorn is a real athlete. Incredibly fast, it can reach speeds of up to 50 miles per hour (50-70 Km/h) over long distances. It can achieve this because its heart and lungs are large and can get more oxygen to the muscles.

Why does the ostrich hide its head in the sand?

To be correct, ostriches don't hide their head in the sand. Since their head is quite small compared to its body, when they lower it to the ground, if observed from afar, it can give the impression that their head is buried in the sand.

Why does the ostrich eat stones?

Ostriches have no teeth and cannot chew. By swallowing small stones and pebbles, they manage to grind the food when it reaches their muscular stomach, which, by contracting, makes the stones (called gastroliths) beat together, so the meal is reduced to a pulp.

Why do ostrich chicks "go to kindergarten"?

The male ostrich builds a nest by digging a shallow hole. His mate and all the other females nearby lay their eggs inside this hole. Up to 300 chicks can be born in this nest and are raised and protected by two parents only.

Why does the milky eagle owl sometimes pretend to be hurt?

Sometimes the milky eagle owl puts on a real show. It flaps its wings and drags itself along, as if it can no longer fly. This is the trick it uses to distract a predator that gets too close to the nest. It makes the predator think that the owl is easy prey, but as soon as it is far enough away, the owl takes off.

Why does the bullfrog create a cocoon around itself?

As with all frogs, its skin is exposed. To prevent it from drying out in the heat of the savanna, the bullfrog buries itself underground, first taking care to wrap itself in a layer of mucus, which, when hardened, becomes a cocoon. The frog can wait for the rain inside the cocoon for up to 7 years.

Why do swallows migrate?

In spring, swallows move to the Northern Hemisphere because they find many insects to eat and few predators for their young ones. When winter arrives and the insects hibernate, they move south to the warm African savanna to avoid starving.

Why does the hippo have eyes, ears, and nostrils on top of its head?

The hippo spends the hot hours of the day almost totally immersed in the water of rivers and lakes. The position of its eyes, ears, and nostrils right on the top of its head allows the hippo to breathe and keep everything that happens around it under control.

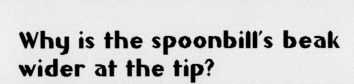

Why is the spoonbill's beak wider at the tip?

The strange beak of this water bird is flat and widens at the tip. This final portion is particularly sensitive, and when the beak hits an object that is moving in the water, the jaws close at great speed and the prey can be captured.

Why are flamingos pink?

They would actually be gray were it not for their particular diet based on small crustaceans and microscopic algae that contain natural dyes capable of coloring the feathers pink.

Why does the platypus have a beak?

The beak of this mammal is different from that of birds: it is flexible and covered with a very sensitive skin that helps the animal to find food underwater.

Why does the pangolin curl up into a ball?

Pangolins are mammals almost entirely covered with hard, overlapping scales. When threatened by a predator, they quickly roll up to form a ball.

Why is the black mamba so called?

Although its body is green, this snake is called "black" because when it is frightened, it opens its mouth wide, revealing the dark spot inside it. The message is clear: go away or I'll kill you with my poisonous bite!

Why do wild dogs hunt in packs?

African wild dogs love to live in large groups of up to 40 individuals who help one another. Collaboration happens mainly during hunting, when the group, led by the pack leader, is able to capture even very large prey.

Why do vultures have bare necks?

It is a matter of cleanliness. Vultures feed on carcasses and sometimes need to stick their heads inside a dead body. By doing this, the feathers on the head and neck would become dirty or could get entangled in something.

Why is termite work important?

These small insects play a fundamental role because, by eating wood, they bring the nutrients from dead plants back to the soil and recycle them, making them available for other creatures.

Why does the aardvark have strong nails?

This great eater of ants and termites has strong claws on the toes of its front legs, which it uses to break the hard walls of termite mounds and eat the occupants, and to dig its den, which it frequently abandons to make a new one.

Why are galagos called "bush babies"?

The galago is a small monkey with large round eyes reminiscent of those of newborn humans, and it also communicates with its peers with a sound very similar to the cry of a small child.

Why does the hyena laugh?

The hyena's "laugh" is actually a way of communicating emotions, such as the excitement of hunting or fear.

Why do bison often roll in the dust?

Bison often lie down and roll around in the dirt to remove ticks and flies that bite them, and to help the shedding of their winter fur. Males also roll about to release their scent and to show off their physical strength.

Why do prairie dogs bark?

These rodents have loud voices that resemble dog barking. Living in a group, they must be able to communicate with all the other members of their numerous colony, especially to signal the arrival of a predator that could surprise a distracted companion.

Why do horses sleep standing up?

Sleeping standing up allows the horse to be ready to escape in case of danger! Horses are able to do this thanks to tendons and ligaments that lock the major joints of their legs. This way the animal relaxes without worrying about falling over.

Why is the cattle egret so called?

Cattle egrets exploit large mammals to feed effortlessly: they follow the animals and capture the insects that rise from the ground as they pass.

Why do prairie dogs build their lairs underground?

For prairie dogs, digging an underground lair is challenging: it involves building numerous chambers connected by long tunnels to form almost a labyrinth. An underground lair, however, is useful because it provides some protection from predators.

53

Why do bees make honey?

Honey is made from the nectar of flowers and is produced by bees to be stored in the hive as food. It is used in the winter months when there are no flowers around to collect nectar from.

Why do fireflies glow?

A firefly glows to get a female's attention. The male illuminates and flashes his abdomen, and when the female sees him shine in that particular way, she responds with her light and accepts him as a companion.

Why do mosquitoes suck blood?

Although it is thought to be for feeding, in reality, mosquitoes feed on sugary juices, such as nectar and honeydew. Only females, for a certain period of their life, sting humans, because only by sucking blood can they develop their eggs.

Why are wasps yellow and black?

The color of the wasps is a warning sign to those who threaten them. Predators know that this color means danger and that they could risk a painful sting if they attempt to catch the wasp!

Why is it called a praying mantis?

Because it holds its front legs in a position that makes it look like it is praying.

Why does the praying mantis devour its mate?

This doesn't always happen. Generally, the female feeds on the male when she has no other food available, and she has to worry about staying strong and being able to survive at least until the moment of laying the eggs and giving birth to her young.

Why does the secretary bird have long, stout legs?

This bird's legs are long because it moves mainly on foot among the tall grasses of the savanna. They are also robust because they are the weapon with which it captures prey, such as snakes, which it tramples until they are dead or stunned enough to be swallowed.

Why does the kingsnake fearlessly prey on rattlesnakes?

Kingsnakes, which are not poisonous, have developed the ability to resist the venom of other snakes. This allows them to attack and eat animals that would surely be indigestible to other predators.

Why do flies buzz?

In addition to the pair of wings they use to fly, flies—as well as mosquitoes—have two tiny shortened wings, called rockers, useful for giving them balance during take-off and landing. These smaller wings vibrate during flight, producing the annoying buzz.

Why do lizards lose their tails?

When a lizard is attacked by a predator, it voluntarily and painlessly detaches its tail, which continues to move, distracting the attacker for long enough to let the lizard escape. The tail grows back a little shorter after a few months.

Water World

In the waters of the seas and oceans,
from the surface to the depth of the
abyss, live the largest, most colorful,
and most bizarre creatures on Earth.

There are those that breathe with gills
and those that breathe with lungs,
those that live fixed to the seabed,
those that swim at various speeds,
and those, like the jellyfish, that instead
let themselves be carried away by the
currents.

Along the coasts and on the shores of
lakes and rivers, you can find animals
that depend on water for survival.
They lay their eggs in it, like frogs,
or they get food from it, like pelicans.

Why does the swordfish have a sword?

The sword is made up of very elongated mouth bones and is used by the swordfish to catch its prey. It chases them not to stab them, but to hit them violently and stun them.

Why do some fish fly?

Some fish have large fins that extend and stiffen to propel themselves out of the water and glide through the air for several seconds. They can also do a row of long leaps thanks to the vibrating movement of the tail. With this technique they can easily escape predators.

Why can the crab stay out of the water for a long time?

Crabs have gills to breathe, like fish, but they can stay out of the water for a long time (and some species never get in). Their secret? They have plates above the gills that seal them, keeping them wet and therefore functional.

Why does the pelican have a bag under its beak?

On the underside of their beak, pelicans have an elastic skin pouch. It is a kind of bag for catching small fish, which get trapped in it. Before being able to swallow the fish, the pelican must let out the collected water, by slightly opening its beak.

Why do oysters produce pearls?

By forming a pearl, oysters put in place a natural defense against an irritating foreign body, such as a grain of sand or a parasite, which has accidentally entered the shell. By wrapping it in layers of mother-of-pearl, very smooth to the touch, they prevent their delicate body from being damaged.

Why does the hermit crab live in a shell?

The abdomen of the hermit crab is soft and delicate and therefore needs protection. For this reason, the crab looks for an empty shell and occupies it, slipping inside, but leaving the claws exposed. It then wanders with the shell on its back, ready to change it when it gets too small.

Why do leatherback turtles have so many teeth?

Inside the leatherback turtle's mouth, there are hundreds of small, pointed teeth. Because it feeds on jellyfish, the turtle can hold on to the soft prey with its teeth and prevent the prey from escaping.

Why do marine iguanas sneeze?

They often ingest a large amount of salt water. To avoid harm to their body, they have to remove the salt from their blood, but not the water! The most practical way to do this is through powerful and frequent sneezing.

Why does the jellyfish sting?

Jellyfish are very simple creatures. To catch prey that is much faster than they are, they must first stun it. They do this with a stinging substance contained in special cells of their tentacles. On contact, these cells "shoot" a small poisonous harpoon.

Why do sea turtles lay their eggs on the beach?

In order to develop, embryos must breathe air through the porous shell, which they could not do if the eggs were immersed in water.

Why does the puffer fish swell?

The puffer fish normally looks like a very ordinary fish, but if it feels threatened, it will start swallowing water to inflate its body. It swells up to 5 times bigger than normal and becomes so big and round that it's difficult to swallow.

Why does the anglerfish have a light above its head?

In the depths of the ocean lives a fish with a huge head: it is the anglerfish. It spends its life perpetually in the dark where the sun's rays do not reach. However, the anglerfish has its own light on its backbone, which functions as a lure to attract prey.

Why does the dolphin make clicking sounds?

It is known that a dolphin whistles to communicate with its fellow dolphins, but sometimes its sound is a noise that resembles a "click" to our ear. By producing a series of clicks, the dolphin can understand what its environment is like, based on the echo that comes back to it.

Why do they say that the limulus is a living fossil?

Looks can be deceiving! Limuli are not related to shrimps and lobsters, but rather to spiders and scorpions. These strange animals roamed the seabed as early as 450 million years ago. This means they were already on Earth before the appearance of the dinosaurs, which we know of only as fossils!

Why does the sperm whale produce ambergris?

Sperm whales are great eaters of cuttlefish and squid, which have a hard beak that is difficult to digest. Inside the intestine, the beaks compact and turn into a solid substance called ambergris. Ambergris is used to make perfumes.

Why do gray whales head to the Caribbean in winter?

With the arrival of winter, gray whales leave the icy waters of the Arctic Ocean and, after a journey of thousands of miles, reach the calm and warm Caribbean Sea, off the coast of Mexico. Here they find the ideal conditions to give birth.

Why does the sperm whale spray from the head?

The sperm whale breathes with its lungs. On its head it has a blowhole, which works like a nostril, to inhale and exhale air. When the whale emerges from the water, no water actually comes out of the blowhole, only air, which condenses into a cloud, just like your breath on a cold day.

Why do humpback whales sing?

The song of a male humpback whale is a combination of many sounds: whistles, grunts, moans. It serves to get noticed by a female and to communicate its position and route.

Why does the whale have no teeth?

It depends on what they eat. Whales feed on very small animals, which they capture in large quantities. Teeth would not be useful for doing this, so instead whales have baleen, a system of long and resistant filaments that function as a filter.

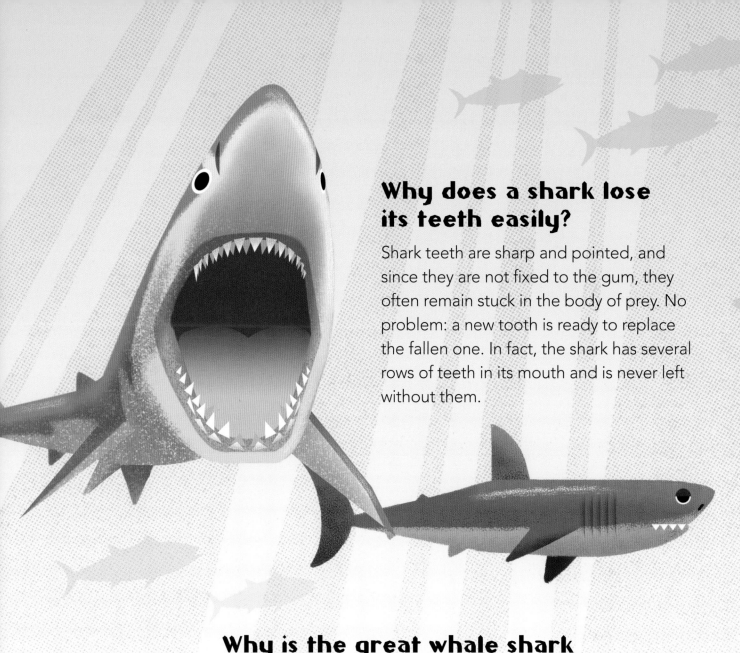

Why does a shark lose its teeth easily?

Shark teeth are sharp and pointed, and since they are not fixed to the gum, they often remain stuck in the body of prey. No problem: a new tooth is ready to replace the fallen one. In fact, the shark has several rows of teeth in its mouth and is never left without them.

Why is the great whale shark considered harmless?

This shark has over 3,000 teeth, but they are tiny in size, no bigger than the head of a matchstick. Their purpose is neither to tear nor to chew. In fact, whale sharks are filter feeders and feed exclusively on tiny organisms, such as plankton.

Why is the killer whale called "killer"?

The orca, like many other animals, is a predator. Its hunting method is particularly aggressive and allows the orca to capture even very large prey. It is likely that the nickname was given in the ancient past by sailors who saw the orca in action.

Why is the hammerhead shark so called?

The name of this shark, with its eyes widely spaced, capable of seeing everything that happens around it, clearly derives from the curious shape of its head, which recalls the shape of a carpenter's club. It is so large that it allows us to recognize the shark immediately.

Why does the manta ray have two horns?

Actually they are not horns, but fins placed on the sides of its head. They are very flexible and can be rolled up while swimming. If, on the other hand, they are unrolled and clearly visible, it means that the ray is looking for food and is using them to channel the plankton toward its mouth.

Why do cuttlefish spray ink?

The ink sprayed on an attacker is a cuttlefish's technique to prepare for escape. The black cloud that forms in the water is used as "smoke in the eyes," and not only does it confuse the predator but it also prevents the predator from seeing the direction taken by the fleeing cuttlefish.

Why does the starfish have no eyes?

Unlike most animals, starfish do not have a head that carries the sense organs. However, they have very simple ocelli on the tip of each arm. Although they do not see the details of things, they can distinguish between light and dark.

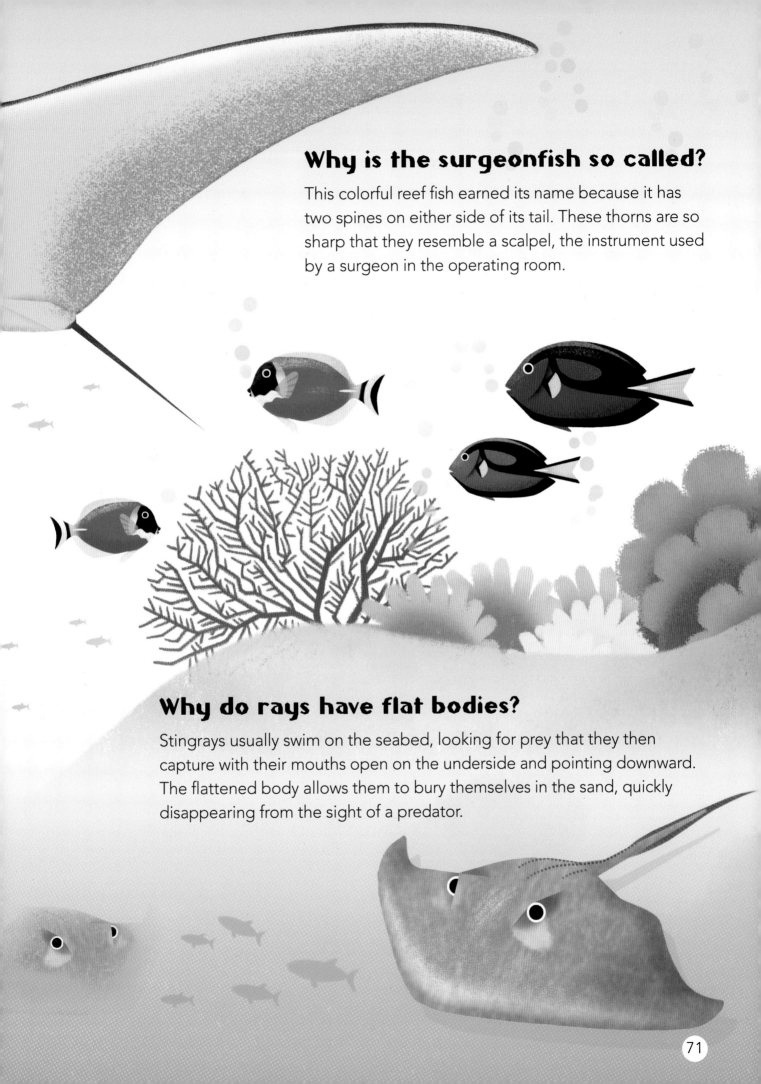

Why is the surgeonfish so called?

This colorful reef fish earned its name because it has two spines on either side of its tail. These thorns are so sharp that they resemble a scalpel, the instrument used by a surgeon in the operating room.

Why do rays have flat bodies?

Stingrays usually swim on the seabed, looking for prey that they then capture with their mouths open on the underside and pointing downward. The flattened body allows them to bury themselves in the sand, quickly disappearing from the sight of a predator.

Why does the moray eel always have its mouth open?

The moray eel opens its mouth and shows its teeth, but not as a sign of threat. It is simply breathing. Unlike other fish, it has to forcefully pump water through its gills to have oxygen, continuously opening and closing its mouth.

Why does the octopus change color?

Few people know that the octopus is a master of disguise. When a predator shows up, the octopus changes the colors of its skin, and in a short time, it disappears, merging with the seabed, becoming indistinguishable from rocks and corals.

Why does the electric eel produce electrical discharges?

The electric eel searches for its prey by swimming slowly. Having no teeth, it puts in place an ingenious system for the capture. It is in fact capable of producing short electric discharges, strong enough to stun those who come within range and easily eat them.

Why do clownfish live in sea anemones?

Clownfish know that the sea anemone stings, but they are not afraid of it because they are immune to its poison, thanks to a special mucus that covers their body. What place could be safer for them? No predator dares to approach the anemones tentacles.

Why does the seahorse have a pouch?

It is the male who takes care of the eggs, protecting them in a leather sac in the abdomen. This pouch can hold over 100 eggs, protected in a liquid that gives them nourishment. When they hatch, the father lets the little ones out of the pouch as in childbirth.

Why does the sea otter hit its chest with stones?

Its diet includes clams and mussels, which have very hard shells. When the otter re-emerges after its catch on the seabed, it lets itself float belly up and uses its chest as a support base, beating stones on the shells to crush them.

Why do cormorants have webbed feet?

Many of the birds related to the aquatic environment must be able to swim well. To be able to move quickly, they need to move the water backward in order to thrust forward. The webbed feet allow the cormorant to give greater strength to the thrust and consequently to advance more easily.

Why do catfish have "whiskers"?

The whiskers of the catfish are called barbels. They are an indispensable aid for getting around in dark waters. They are also used to find food by touching it and even tasting it. The whiskers are therefore important sense organs, without which the catfish could not live.

Why do salmon swim up rivers?

When breeding time comes, the salmon leaves the sea and begins to swim up river on a journey that will take it back to where it was born. Here, before dying, it will lay its eggs. In the fresh, shallow water, the eggs and young will be safe from predators.

Why do sea snakes have flat tails?

Living in marine waters, these snakes, unlike their relatives that crawl on the ground, move around by swimming. This is why they have a flat tail in the shape of an oar. This feature makes for more agile and faster movement in the water, even if it is very clumsy on land.

Perennial Ice and High Mountains

The regions of Earth where ice covers the ground and it is cold all year round are truly inhospitable places, yet they, too, are home to many animals.

To be able to survive here, the bare minimum an animal needs is a thick layer of fat or even warm fur, preferably as white as snow.

In the high mountains, life is just as hard. In addition to facing freezing temperatures, especially in winter, animals risk falls, and since there is little oxygen in the air, it is also difficult to breathe.

Why doesn't the polar bear slide on ice?

Under the sole of its paws are black pads of thick skin, covered with small, soft skin bumps that prevent the bear from falling.

Why do seals make holes in the ice?

With the arrival of the cold season, the Arctic Sea begins to freeze. Seals make holes in the ice and, from time to time, pop out to breathe. It is a dangerous time for the seal as it could fall victim to a polar bear.

Why do seals never drink?

Living in the sea, seals have a lot of water available but it is salty and not good for quenching their thirst. For this reason, they drink it only occasionally, and for their daily needs they use the liquids present in the food they eat.

Why is the polar bear's fur not white, but colorless?

The white color you see is due to a trick of the light. In reality, its fur is transparent, as it is hollow and full of air. This particular fur lets the mild heat of the sun through, which reaches the black skin, from which it is absorbed. With this trick, the bear stays warmer.

Why are Arctic seal pups white?

The pups of the Arctic seal are born with long, fluffy white fur. In addition to insulating the body from the ice they lie on, the fur helps them stay warm until they have developed a thick layer of fat, which happens after about three to four weeks.

Why do male hooded seals have a ball-shaped head?

The adult males have a "hood" on their head between their nose and eyes. When the hood is deflated, it hangs over the upper lip, while when seals get angry or want to impress a female, the hood is inflated and protrudes from one of the nostrils.

Why does the emperor penguin fast throughout winter?

Winter, which begins in June in the Southern Hemisphere, is the breeding season for emperor penguins. The female lays a single egg and entrusts it to the male, who will have to keep it warm for two months prior to hatching, keeping it balanced on his feet. During this time, he has no way to eat anything.

Why is the penguin unable to fly?

Penguins are birds that live in the sea. Their wings are moved by very powerful pectoral muscles but are unsuitable for flight. Short and robust, they are fin-shaped. The body, although heavy, is hydrodynamic so the animal can move in the water with great agility, as if it were flying.

Why doesn't the blood of many Southern Ocean fish freeze?

The waters of the Arctic Ocean are cold enough to freeze the blood in your veins! However, this does not happen to the fish that live there because they have special substances in their blood that work as antifreeze, preventing them from turning into icicles.

Why do penguins
sway when they walk?

Penguins are birds that swim like fish, but, having short legs and webbed feet, it is very tiring for them to walk. By swinging when they walk, they get less tired.

Why does the narwhal have a tusk on its nose?

The tusk, which can exceed 8 feet (2,5 m) in length, is actually a canine tooth that protrudes out of the mouth. It is found only in males and may serve to attract the attention of females and frighten rival males.

Why do walruses have long teeth?

They are a defense against predators, and when sunk into floating ice, they help pull the heavy body of the walrus out of the water. Males also show them off to conquer a female.

Why do walruses have a mustache?

The mustache, called "whiskers," are very sensitive and are used by walruses to find prey in the depth of the sea, where there is little light. Approaching with their snout to the bottom of the sea, they spray water from their nostrils to easily discover the mollusks buried in the mud.

Why does the Arctic fox have small ears?

The small size of the ears prevents the fox from losing heat. Although tiny, the ears allow it to perfectly hear prey hidden in the snow.

Why does the Arctic fox have a very bushy tail?

The Arctic fox has to come up with a thousand ways to protect itself from the cold. The thick white tail, for example, is very useful for hiding when it sleeps in the snow because it wraps around the body, hiding the eyes and black nose. Plus, it also works as a warm blanket.

Why does the common shag spend a long time on shore with its wings spread?

Shags are birds that specialize in sea fishing, which is why they dive into the water to chase and catch the fish that make up their meal. Once out of the water, however, they are all soaked and therefore need to dry their feathers.

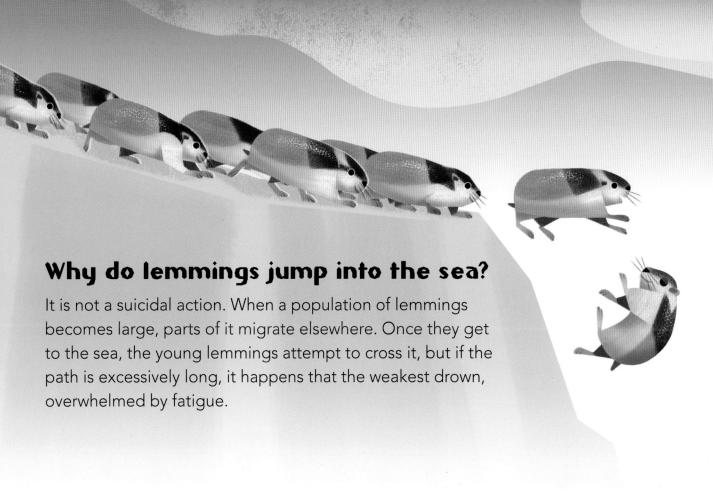

Why do lemmings jump into the sea?

It is not a suicidal action. When a population of lemmings becomes large, parts of it migrate elsewhere. Once they get to the sea, the young lemmings attempt to cross it, but if the path is excessively long, it happens that the weakest drown, overwhelmed by fatigue.

Why does the puffin have a colorful beak?

Puffins live on the northern coasts. During the freezing winter, their triangular beak has a dull hue, but in spring, when it's time to look for a partner, the beak turns orange, yellow, and blue, making them more attractive.

Why is the elephant seal so called?

These large seals have earned their name for their proboscis, which only adult males possess. It is used to enhance their cry, consisting of loud roaring sounds, produced especially in the mating season, when there is great competition for the conquest of females.

Why does guillemots lay pear-shaped eggs?

Guillemots make their nest on the cliffs in very crowded colonies. The pear shape of the egg reduces the risk of rolling and increases the strength of the shell. The particular shape also helps the egg to keep itself "cleaner" since the more rounded part always remains above the dirt.

Why can the Tibetan antelope breathe well even at high altitudes?

In the high mountains, air is thinner and therefore there is less oxygen for breathing. However, Tibetan antelopes have wide nostrils that contain inflatable air sacs, with which they improve their breathing at high altitudes. For this reason, their snouts appear quite swollen.

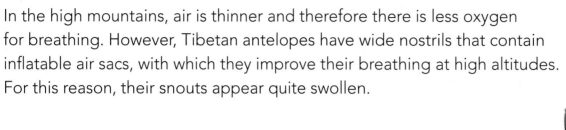

Why does the mountain gorilla beat its chest?

Adult male gorillas hit themselves on the chest to attract females and scare away potential rivals. They don't really punch themselves, but rather cup their hands, so as to increase the sound, which can be heard over a mile away.

Why doesn't the slow worm have legs?

Although it can be easily confused with snakes, the slow worm is actually a lizard with no legs. It spends much of its time digging in the ground and among decomposing vegetation, and its limbs would get in the way of its movement.

Why does the llama spit?

This is not about rudeness. Llamas spit on each other when irritated or frightened. Females spit to alienate males who are of no interest to them. When a lama spits on a person, it is treating the person in the same way as it treats its fellow llamas.

Why can yaks live in the highest mountains?

Yaks are large cattle that normally live above 13,000 feet (4,000 m) in the Himalayan mountains, the highest peaks in the world. They can breathe the oxygen-poor air of these altitudes because they have powerful hearts and lungs, three times the size of those of other cattle.

Why don't plateau pikas hibernate?

These little relatives of rabbits make it through the freezing winter months without hibernating thanks to an unexpected resource. In addition to eating flowers and wild plants stored in burrows during summer, they eat the poop of yaks—the large cattle of the mountains—thereby combating the lack of food, typical of the winter months.

Why does the rock ptarmigan dig a hole in the snow?

In the winter season, when the cold is very intense, the ptarmigan exploits the insulating power of the snow by digging cozy burrows under the snow, where it can rest and enjoy a little more warmth than the harsh outside temperatures.

Why does the snow leopard have a thick, flexible, and very long tail?

The tail of the snow leopard is essential to give balance when the leopard jumps between cliffs. It also allows it to maneuver quickly and comes in handy for correcting the direction of travel while the leopard chases prey that escapes by zigzagging.

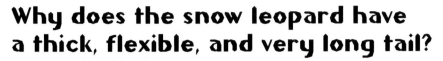

Why does the bearded vulture eat bones?

Carcass bones are the main food of this scavenger bird. It might seem like an unappetizing meal, but it is certainly easy to find because it is overlooked by other animals. The vulture's gastric juices digest bones in less than 24 hours.

Why are the golden eagle's newborns covered in a soft duvet?

The chicks are born in a nest leaning against a rocky wall and they must be protected from the cold when the parents are away. The fluffy duvet keeps them warm. Eaglets change their feathers several times before leaving the nest at the age of 5-6 months.

Why does the caribou migrate to the tundra?

The long move toward the north takes place in spring, when the young are to be born. The tundra is indeed a safe place for babies because there are fewer predators there. In addition, newly sprouted plants are abundant and very nutritious, especially for new mothers who have to breastfeed.

Why do eagles have excellent eyesight?

An eagle sees 4-5 times better than humans. It has very sensitive eyes, which send richly detailed images to the brain. This excellent vision is important in hunting, to identify prey from above, before swooping down to catch it.

Why do reindeer have large hooves fringed with fur?

Walking in the snow can be difficult. The reindeer, however, has large feet with two toes equipped with robust and wide hooves, which distribute the body weight, preventing the reindeer from sinking. They are a bit like snowshoes embedded into the feet.

Why do reindeer's eyes turn blue in winter?

Reindeer eye color changes with the seasons.
In summer, when the sun is high in the sky and the days are bright, the eyes appear gold. In winter, however, they become less reflective, until they become dark blue, to allow them to see in the lowest light.

Why does the chamois have a beard on its back?

A stripe of fur called a "beard" runs along the entire back of adult males, formed by long dark hairs that in autumn can reach 8 inches (20 cm) in length. The chamois can lift its beard to appear larger in the eyes of a predator or a rival.

Why are musk ox calves not afraid of wolves?

The little ones can count on help from their elders. If a pack of wolves surrounds the herd, the musk oxen form a circle, turning their thick, pointed horns toward the wolves. The calves are safe within this defensive fortress, which is practically impenetrable.

Why is the snow owl white?

White is a camouflage color that allows the owl to hide in its environment—the polar ice and the tundra—where everything is covered by snow for many months. In reality, only the male is completely white, while the female always has a few brown feathers.

Why does the ermine change color?

In the mountains, where ermines are widespread, winter snow falls abundantly and whitens the whole landscape. In order to hide, ermines gradually change their fur—which in summer is red-brown—and become white. Only the tip of the tail remains black.

Why are musk oxen so called?

Musk oxen inhabit the icy lands of the Arctic. Their name comes from their resemblance to cows and oxen—although they are not relatives at all—and from the strong musky smell produced by males to attract females.

Why don't ibexes slip over steep slopes?

Ibex feet have two toes that they spread apart to increase their balance. Furthermore, under the hooves, there are rough but soft pads, which grip the rock, allowing ibexes to climb almost vertical walls without the risk of falling into ravines.

Why do ibexes often climb south-facing slopes?

Even in the winter months, the ibex lives 6,500 feet (2000 m) above sea level. In the morning, it must try to warm up quickly, so it tends to choose the mountain slopes sheltered from the wind and south facing, because they are the ones most illuminated by the sun and therefore warmer.

Why does the mountain goat lick rocks?

A mountain goat's meal consists of woody plants, herbs, pieces of bark, moss, and lichen. Sometimes, however, it also licks the rocks because they contain mineral salts of which the goat is particularly fond. Salt represents an important element of its diet.

Why does the viper have a poisonous bite?

As in all poisonous snakes, the viper's venom serves to kill prey and injure attackers, but it also helps its stomach by aiding the breakdown of prey—which is swallowed whole—thereby making digestion easier.

THE AUTHOR

Cristina Banfi is a graduate in natural sciences from the University of Milan. She has taught at various schools, and for over twenty years, she has been working in the fields of scientific communication and teaching through play for children.

THE ILLUSTRATOR

Lorenzo Sabbatini is a freelance illustrator for various world-class publishing houses and advertising agencies. Since 2006, he has been a member of the Italian Association of Illustrators.

WS whitestar kids™ is a trademark of White Star s.r.l.

© 2022 White Star s.r.l.
Piazzale Luigi Cadorna, 6
20123 Milan, Italy
www.whitestar.it

Translation: Inga Sempel
Editing: Abby Young

Second printing, March 2024

ISBN 978-88-544-1913-1
  2 3 4 5 6   28 27 26 25 24

Printed and manufactured in China by
Leo Paper Products, Kowloon Bay, Kowloon, Hong Kong

FSC
www.fsc.org

MIX
Paper from
responsible sources
FSC® C178000